Peter is shipwrecked on an island where he finds a dragon, and they set out to help each other find their way home...

The Dragon
and the Island

A Bedtime Story

by Valerie Hazell
illustrated by Gill Guile

Copyright © 1989 by World International Publishing Limited.
All rights reserved.
Published in Great Britain by World International Publishing Limited,
An Egmont Company, Egmont House, P.O.Box 111,
Great Ducie Street, Manchester M60 3BL.
Printed in DDR. ISBN 0 7235 1266 3

A CIP catalogue record for this book is available from the British Library

It had been such a lovely, sunny day and Peter had taken his father's small boat out to sea to do some fishing.

But black clouds had suddenly rolled across the sun and a terrible storm had blown up.

Peter struggled with all his might to control the little boat, but the storm was too strong.

When a big wave hit the boat, Peter was knocked into the sea, and he was washed to an island far away.

"I must find out where I've come to," said Peter. "And I must try to find my way home."

Peter walked along the beach towards a wood.

Inside the wood Peter found the strangest building he had ever seen.

It was a small palace which was all in ruins. As he moved closer he could see carvings of dragons on the walls, and the handle on a big door was even shaped like a dragon's head.

Peter turned the handle and the door opened. Summoning up all his courage, he went inside.

Suddenly, a voice called out.

"I've been waiting for you," it said sadly, "for more than a thousand years."

Peter was startled. He could hardly believe what he saw. For in the palace was a green dragon.

"Please don't stare at me. It's rude," said the dragon.

"Sorry," said Peter. "But I've never seen a dragon before."

"I'm the last dragon in the world," said the dragon. "And I've been on this island for a very long time. A wicked magician put me here and made my wings useless. All I want to do is fly away home."

"Did you say *island*?" asked Peter, nervously. "I'm shipwrecked and I want to go home too."

"Don't worry," said the dragon. "I'm sure we can help each other."

And then he started to tell Peter all about himself and the time when he lived in a distant country.

Peter listened, spellbound.

"I travelled all over the world. But once when I returned home I was naughty," said the dragon.

The dragon hung his head and looked ashamed.

"In the middle of a royal wedding I did some flame throwing and burnt the chief magician's best trousers. He was furious and he cast a spell which made my wings useless. Then I was banished to this island, where I must stay until the power is returned to my wings."

The dragon began to cry and big tears rolled down his green face.

Peter held his paw and said, "Please don't cry, I shall help you to fly again."

"I've been waiting for more than a thousand years for someone to help me," the dragon replied. "If you can help me fly home, then I will help you too."

Peter looked happy, and the dragon stopped crying.

"Tomorrow I will tell you how to help me," the dragon said to Peter.

Next day, Peter and the green dragon set off through the wood.

"To make my wings work again you must rub my back with magic ointment," the dragon explained.

"That's easy," said Peter.

"It's not *that* easy," replied the dragon. "The ointment is in a jar at the bottom of a deep well."

When they reached the well Peter looked down in dismay. It was impossible to see anything.

"Whatever shall we do?" gasped Peter.

Peter and the dragon sat down beside the well, and started to think of a plan. The dragon looked quite sad.

"I know!" shouted Peter. "If the jar has a handle, I can reach it with my fishing rod."

The dragon put his strong arms around Peter and held him carefully. Peter lowered his hook into the deep well.

After an hour of fishing in the well, Peter began to think there was no handle on the jar after all.

But just as he was going to give up, he felt something on the hook. Peter was so excited that he pulled it up too quickly, and it fell off and sank to the bottom again.

The dragon looked very sad.

"I'm sorry," said Peter. "I'll try again."

It took another hour before Peter caught it again. This time he pulled it up with the greatest care.

"It's the jar!" called Peter.

The green dragon was so happy that he blew a puff of white smoke.

Peter caught the jar with his hand and showed it to the dragon.

"Thank you, thank you," said the dragon, hugging Peter tighter than ever. "Now let's see if the magic ointment really works!"

Peter took the lid off the jar and put some of the ointment on his fingers. Then, trembling, he rubbed the ointment over the dragon's green back.

At first nothing happened.

But then all at once the dragon's wings stood out firm and strong.

"It's worked!" shouted Peter and the dragon at the same time. And they did a little dance together because they were both so happy.

"Jump on my back," called the dragon. "We're going home!"

To their great delight they were soon flying across the sea, leaving the island far behind them.

"This is a wonderful feeling," said Peter.

Soon they reached the mainland and the dragon set Peter down on the beach near to his house.

It was a sad moment when Peter
and the dragon said goodbye to
each other. But not too sad because
Peter was happy to be home again
and his friend the dragon could fly
once more.

The dragon flew high up into the
sky, and Peter waved until he was
no more than a tiny speck in the
distance.

Peter picked up his fishing rod
and looked out to sea at where the
island used to be.

It had completely disappeared!